"How Did You Manage That?"

"How Did You Manage That?"

A Manager's Guide To Doing It Right

Jim Weaver

Writers Club Press
New York Lincoln Shanghai

"How Did You Manage That?"
A Manager's Guide To Doing It Right

All Rights Reserved © 2002 by Jim Weaver

Writers Club Press
an imprint of iUniverse, Inc.

For information address:
iUniverse
2021 Pine Lake Road, Suite 100
Lincoln, NE 68512
www.iuniverse.com

ISBN: 0-595-25603-1 (Pbk)
ISBN: 0-595-65204-2 (Cloth)

Printed in the United States of America

Preface

Over 13 years ago, a commercial oil tanker carrying millions of gallons of oil ran aground on Bligh Reef negligently resulting in the spillage of the equivalent of 125 Olympic swimming pools (11 million gallons) of oil into the biologically rich waters of Prince William Sound. Fingers pointed in every direction accusing lack of talent, improper maneuverability, excessive fatigue, alcohol impairment, insufficient crew members, and ineffective vessel traffic systems. Regardless of who was to blame, it was clear that the inability to manage a critical situation resulted in disastrous consequences.

Management's one responsibility is the competent control of human resources. If this occurs, so does productivity. If it does not occur, management cannot legitimately claim to be successful regardless of its level of talent.

In a "backhanded" way, this book is about good management. It pokes fun at management misfits, although I realize all too well that they are the purveyors of untold subordinate frustration and distress. I am constantly amazed that, not only do they exist, but they permeate almost every organization, regardless of its size or function. They are quickly identified by some or all of the following immutable characteristics:

- They never were, are not now, nor ever will be competent to take the organizational helm.

• They might even qualify as absolute idiots.

• They reserve the credit for themselves and assign blame to everyone else.

• Every time they see a spotlight, they jump into it and start dancing.

• Their thought processes are muddled, and their creativity is A.W.O.L.

• They can't decide whether to make a decision or not.

• They are very "activity" oriented, but haven't got a clue as to "accomplishment."

• They find great comfort in organizational stagnation, but cower when faced with any type of organizational movement.

• They continue to talk long after their ideas have run out.

• Their political motto is, "Win at all costs, take no prisoners, and step on a few heads along the way."

• Like athlete's foot, they never go away.

This book will do little to rectify the damage caused by these dumbbells. They'll never read it and wouldn't think it referred to them if they did. But you **are** reading it. Maybe it's because you aspire to management at some future time and are looking for ways to do it properly. I sincerely hope so. Pay close attention to the section called, "Managing to do it right." We don't need anymore misfits out there messing things up. I would hope that in some way this book contributes to your management success. How will you know? Because subordinates will experience your management style and instead of asking, "how did you manage that?", they'll say you're "managing to do it right."

Acknowledgements

I would like to express my appreciation to Ray Weaver for his creativity and manuscript enhancement efforts. Molly Lagatta invested hours and energy into proofreading and polishing the initial and final drafts. Without the dedication of these two people, this work would have been much more difficult. My wife, Karin, and my daughter, Jessica, provided continual support and helped to keep me on task. Finally, I would like to thank the long list of managers, peers, and subordinates who worked with me and contributed to my own management education. You know who you are. To all of you my heartfelt thanks.

Contents

CHAPTER ONE

Idiots At The Helm

"*Even as he walks along the road, the fool lacks sense and shows everyone how stupid he is.* Ecclesiastes 10:3 The Holy Bible (NIV)

Bureaucrat\'byur-uh-krat\n 1. An official (usually government) who follows a narrow, rigid, formal management routine, and who is established with great authority in his/her own department. 2. A management misfit.

Some people have no business being managers. They may manage to get up in the morning, pour milk on their oatmeal without spilling it, and drive to work without registering a kill on the way. But they are about as functional at managing people as the shipsmate who, when he found out that the Titanic was sinking, ran out and rearranged the deck chairs. Work, by its very nature, is supposed to be a productive exercise. But it is also a social activity. Employees go to work for more reasons than just to make a living. When their work life is made miserable by some nincompoop who has been placed in charge, and has no business being there, they can become unproductive and uncommunicative. In some instances, they even become disloyal and flee to jobs where the pay may not be as high, but the manager is not as stupid.

Management will forever be burdened with a few self-obsessed egomaniacs who have insidiously wiggled their way up the chain of command. How does it happen? How do the people with no management talent rise to positions where they can irritate so many people? It must be a complex process to understand, and difficult to fix, because the practice, like some uncontrollable disease, seems to have permeated the entire work-a-day world from the smallest governmental entities to the largest private industry corporations.

Families, buddies, and political considerations aside, there exists a number of promotional practices and processes which are used to determine who does and does not get promoted to management. Although some practices may be valid, many are not. They claim to be able to identify and scoop the organizational cream from the top. Unfortunately, when the process is complete, the "cream" is neither sweet nor satisfying. The result is a manager who causes heartache and interferes with productivity. Several serious misperceptions contribute to the placement of idiots at the helm. It might serve us well to examine a few.

Misperception #1 If an employee is especially good at a particular job function, it follows that s/he will be equally good as a manager.

Hardly. Workers who get classified as "good employees" are so called because they come to work with positive attitudes, perform their specific job functions well, and display loyalty toward their organization. Management appreciates employees like this and looks for ways to reward them above and beyond salary and annual cost of living increases. If the good employee participates and performs well during promotional selection processes, s/he eventually gets promoted. But, management skill has little to do with individual job function knowledge. Clearly, a working knowledge of the field being managed is necessary, but an above average worker is no shoe-in candidate for a good manager. In some respects, it might even get in the way. For example, if the aggressive worker is promoted to a management position, and his/her new subordinates are not as talented or enthusiastic as s/he is, the new manager may become frustrated with the fact that subordinates don't work at the level of intensity s/he desires—especially if s/he knows little about how to motivate subordinates and lead people. That being the case, the manager has two choices—do the work him/herself, or continually berate the subordinate. Neither is a very effective management option.

Management is a skill in and unto itself. Good workers don't always make good managers. But a good manager can step into any myriad of positions and successfully apply appropriate management techniques that make things work.

Some years back, a local college was looking to open a new police academy. They advertised for an academy director and received applications from a large and varied pool of applicants. One of the candidates who applied for the job was a local government public safety employee with over a decade of management experience in various criminal justice arenas. He was surprised at the interview when the selection committee continued to pepper him with questions about his "training" experience. Finally, he simply said to the committee, "Ladies and gentlemen, I am not a trainer. I understand the components of training and their role in producing professional law enforcement officers. But I am not a teacher. I am a manager. If you are looking for a 'training' professional, I am not your guy. But if you want someone who can insure that your academy runs smoothly, and in accordance with sound, ethical management principles, you need look no further." He got the job. You see, you can lead a horse to water, but you cannot manage him to drink. That is unless you know a little about horses, and a good deal about management.

Misperception #2 Job knowledge is far more important than people skills.

A great motivator once offered an expression which says, "People don't care how much you know, until they know how much you care about them." You cannot be an effective manager unless you understand the importance of the people who work for you. It is, in fact, the most critical skill that you must master. And yet, there are people in management positions who can make employees angry just by saying, "Good Morning." Even  though they say the right words, their expression purports that they were weaned on a dill pickle.

I used to work for a manager who would come into the office and ask how everyone was doing. Once he had spoken to everyone, he would comment in somewhat of a joking manner, "O.K. So much for the sensitivity crap. Now everybody get to work!" Although we saw it for what it was...his feeble attempt at humor, we didn't appreciate it. Many managers come across as unfeeling, even though they ask the right questions and/or use the right words.

As a manager, everything for which you are responsible is generally accomplished through others. This can be extremely satisfying and, at times, equally frustrating. But it is a truism. Subordinates don't give a hoot about how knowledgeable a manager is, if s/he doesn't know how to relate to them from an interpersonal standpoint.

Misperception #3 Formal management training is unnecessary. The new manager will learn as s/he goes along.

Human beings have been training since their introduction to the potty, continuing all the way through some level of formal educational schooling. So why is it that they assume that a promotion is automatically accompanied by some miraculous endowment of managerial knowledge? Of course, they can learn as they go. But, without some prepared, consistent, formal training, they'll step on their own feet, their employees' necks, and will be destined to repeat the mistakes of their predecessors. Essentially because they don't possess a significant amount of managerial knowledge to know they are doing it wrong.

Misperception #4 Workers don't really care who the manager is. They will continue to do their jobs regardless of who's in charge.

Don't kid yourself. "Who's the boss?" is one of the first and foremost questions that employees want answered. Most employees have worked for a lousy manager. In fact, many of them are working for a lousy manager **now**. They realize that the manager may be restricted in what s/he can do **for** them, but that s/he has almost "carte blanche" relative to what s/he can do **to** them. Good managers are able to keep employees' chins up when times are down and noses to the grindstone when additional output is critical. The poor manager not only discourages the workers, s/he actually diminishes productive work. Workers waste time talking about how much they hate him/her as opposed to getting the work done. Oh, intimidation might work for a while, but employees never forget the person who treated them badly. What's more, a poor manager's reputation proceeds him/her. People **very much** care who the boss is. And although employees may continue to work at an acceptable level, the personality, knowledge and sensitivity of the boss will ultimately determine the level of intensity to which worker activity climbs.

Misperception #5 It's only one management position. It can't cause that much damage.

Only one bomb was dropped on Hiroshima. How much damage did **it** do? A dysfunctional manager harms more than the individual work area s/he manages. Organizations are not islands. They are interconnected networks which either prosper or suffer depending upon whether or not individual units do their jobs. It is unfortunate that so many organizations refuse to remove managers from a position once it has been confirmed that they are incompetent practitioners. Instead, the organization either ignores the problem, or more often, runs around behind these losers building artificial support systems to continually prop them up. Most of the management evaluation scores I've ever seen, including my own, started at "excellent" and went up. What message does that send to everyone in the organization? It tells them that the management mooncalf is here to stay regardless of the number of mistakes s/he makes, and despite the number of people who are negatively impacted by his/her presence. Beautiful!

When asked why we did something in a particular way, one of my early manager's favorite responses was, "because we've always done it that way." This is indicative of a bureaucracy going around in circles at warp speed. All of the misperceptions I have related herein bolster that kind of philosophy. Oh, without a doubt it works to feed and nurture the bureaucracy, but it's pot-poor management. And as one frustrated subordinate so eloquently summed up…"The management ostrich who buries his/her head in the organizational sand deserves to have his/her managerial fanny kicked." As it is said, let it be written.

★   **Managing to do it right…**

1. Realize that good management development takes time, training, patience, and practice. It is neither easy nor free.
2. Get some formal management training. Don't make your subordinates suffer while you learn.
3. There's always another way to squeeze the toothpaste. Look for it.
4. Regardless of how smart you are, you cannot manage without people skills.

CHAPTER TWO

...You Might Be An Idiot

"What a waste it is to lose one's mind. Or not to have a mind is being very wasteful. How true that is." Dan Quayle, Vice President

Idiot \'id-e-it \n [ME, fr. L *idiota*] 1. A person affected
with idiocy; esp. a feeble-minded dolt 2. A silly or
foolish person 3. Occasionally, a manager

Doughheaded managers abound. Usually, there is at least one
in every organization. Some organizations, especially in the
public sector, are plagued with a plethora of knotheads who
know about as much regarding management as General
Custer knew about fighting Indians. The scary truth is that
they don't **know** they're idiots. The scarier truth is that they
think they are quite talented at what they do, and they aspire
to even loftier management positions.

If you are a manager, you might be an idiot and not even
know it. Here is your self-directed guide to determining the
degree of your own management lunacy.

1. **If you assume you have the respect of your peers and subordinates just because you got promoted to management…you might be an idiot.** Subordinate respect does
   not automatically accompany your new title. People will
   watch you to be sure, but you will have to **earn** your right
   to respect. If anything, the scrutiny you experience will be
   more severe. The amount of time you spend standing on
   your own two feet versus the amount of time you spend
   pulling them out of your mouth will go a long way to
   define the initial impression you make upon your subordinates.

2. **If you walk around insisting that everyone, including your
   friends and associates, address you by your new title…you**

might be an idiot. Don't kid yourself. The more you act like the new position has changed you, the more you will be disliked. That is, unless you were hated in the first place. If that's the case, go ahead. Nobody likes you worth a darn anyway.

3. **If you make assignments, then disappear so that your subordinates can get no additional direction from you…you might be an idiot.** Occasionally, subordinates need support. They also need encouragement. This is Management 101. But, of course, if you never had any management training, you wouldn't know this. You might also not realize that when you give an employee more than one job to do, you need to assign priorities to the tasks. They are not psychic. Make yourself available for direction and support, then try to stay out of the way.

4. **If you are always missing good opportunities to shut up…you might be an idiot.** Managers who are considered idiots are many times labeled as such because of their proclivity to continue talking long after their ideas have run out. A good management rule of thumb is to keep quiet unless you can improve upon the silence.

5. **If you toss something onto your subordinate's desk five minutes before the close of business, and demand that it be done before s/he goes home…you might be an idiot.** I wish I had a dollar for every secretary or subordinate who detested his/her boss. Believe it or not, they do not consider it a refreshing challenge when you dump things on them at

the last minute. They **do** have a life beyond work. Let them live it.

6. If Dr. Suess's *Yerdle the Turtle* (**read the book**) **is your hero…you might be an idiot.** If I say anymore at this point you won't read the book. It's as good of a management text as presently exists.

7. **If you are totally focused on the end product, resulting in a domineering management style with outbursts of anger, blaming, and lack of respect for your employees…you might be an idiot.** Never forget that the  subordinate holds your fate in his/her hands. You might think you are in charge, but if you persist in this type of management style, your employees will eventually sabotage your intentions, compromise your mission, and give you a dose of management castor oil you won't soon forget.

8. **If all the subordinates who truly respect you can fit into the phone booth across the street…you might be an idiot.** Courtesy costs nothing. Yet it is the number one thing subordinates equate with mutual respect. If you are an inconsiderate boss, you will never gain the respect of others, regardless of how knowledgeable you are.

9. **If your ego is so bloated, you are never willing to take the blame…you might be an idiot.** You are only human. You're going to make mistakes, and some of them will be real boners. Mistakes are forgivable. Refusal to be accountable is not. When you do something wrong, apologize for it, fix it, and try not to repeat it. But don't blame it on others. It doesn't fool anyone.

10. **If your position as a manager is largely due to the fact that a close relative or friend promoted you…you might be an idiot.** Most people are realistic. They understand that from time to time, relationships determine promotions. But if you are where you are based on **who** you know as opposed to **what** you know, be aware that it's no secret. If you are one of these, and you think no one realizes it, you are a loon.

11. **If you make a big deal out of appearance standards, while you, yourself resemble a bag of doorknobs in your clothes…you might be an idiot.** Some managers can put on a $900.00 suit and it will still look like socks on a rooster. Regardless, you still set the standard for those under your employ. As the old adage goes, "don't tell me what you want, show me." You as the manager set the example—not just by how you act, but by how you look. If you come to work looking like the court jester, expect nothing less from your subordinates.

12. **If you like to procrastinate, but seldom get around to it…you might be an idiot.** Bottlenecks ruin projects. The

manager who demands that work be on his/her desk by a
certain time, then allows it to linger in the office forever
and anon, will be despised by those who did the work.
Your job as manager is to keep things moving. Your failure
to do so is frustrating and demeaning to those who got
the work to you on schedule.

13. **If your management vision for the organization can best
be summed up in the two words, "Now what?"…you
might be an idiot.** Flying by the seat of your pants can be
an innovative style under some very restrictive circumstances. However, subordinates generally want to know
where the organization is going and what plans have been
created to get it there. Managers who operate only in the
reactive mode are considered to be in over their head. And
they are.

14. **If you use words like "Scenario-dependent pre-crisis
strategy" instead of "Let's figure out what to do "…you
might be an idiot.** If you can't communicate, you can't
manage. No one cares about the extent of your vocabu-
lary or the amount of jargon you know. If they can't
understand you, they will never know what you want
from them.

15. **If you believe that, with your help, the bureaucracy can
outlast anything meaningful…you might be an idiot.** If
you sense that the perpetuation of the organizational
structure is more important than the work it was created
to do, you would make a perfect civil service manager. In

fact, you probably **are** a civil service manager. Bureaucratic managers are not paid for what they accomplish, but rather for how well they follow the policy manual. What a shame.

★ Managing to do it right…

1. Getting promoted no more makes you a manager than going to a rodeo makes you a cowboy. You must earn respect of others. It is not automatic.
2. As a manager you are constantly on stage. People will either laud you or laugh at you. How you act daily determines their response.
3. The difference between icon and idiot can be summed up in the Golden Rule. Memorize it, and manage your people accordingly.

CHAPTER THREE

If It Works, Take The Credit. If It Breaks, Blame Somebody

"I am not without accomplishment. I have managed to distribute poverty equally." Nguyen Co Thatch, Vietnamese Foreign Minister

> Glory hound\glor-e 'haund\n 1. One who avidly seeks the praise of others. 2. A manager who sees something good happening, and jumps around in front of it to take all the credit.

In 1996, a little 7 year old girl, accompanied by her father and a flight instructor, attempted to set a record by becoming the youngest person to fly a single-engine airplane 7,000 miles from coast to coast. Behind schedule, overloaded, and in a blinding rainstorm, the plane attempted unsuccessfully to take off from a western U.S. airport. Everyone on board was killed. The last words of the child pilot as they took off were, "Look at the rain, look at the rain."

Here's the pertinent question. Who really would have gotten the credit had the little girl been successful? Was it the girl herself? Doubtful. How many of your children have ever verbalized the desire to set a world flying record at age 7? Was it the girl's decision to take off in a dangerous rainstorm just to keep pace with a pre-determined flight schedule? It doesn't take long to realize that the person in charge was the one who stood to gain and made the horrific decisions which resulted in tragedy.

Everyone likes to get credit for doing good things. It is a part of human nature. Conversely, we try to divorce ourselves from activities and projects that appear to be "going south." Nothing wrong with that either. But the manager who takes either of these to the extreme takes unfair advantage of those who are assigned to help him/her complete the task at hand.

In almost every organization there are employees who struggle daily to cope with unreasonable bosses who are too focused on results, and have a general lack of respect for the employee. One stressed-out employee shared with me how her boss walked in just before the close of business and thrust the same group of papers at her for the fourth time in two weeks. His instructions were the same as every time before. "Rework these figures and bring them to me when you're done."

"He's impossible!" she said. "He wants everything done and redone, and it really doesn't matter how inconvenienced I am, or how long it takes as long as he gets credit for the overall product when the job is completed."

When she protested to him about the lateness of the hour, and the amount of time that would be required to accomplish the task, he just got red-faced and shouted, "I need it now!" Then he stormed back into his office.

Managers must get things done through other people. But the relationship need not, and should not be a master-slave situation. Managers who demand that every single thing be done in a perfect way, regardless of the toll it takes on employees, are not pursuing excellence, but are compulsively striving toward unrealistic goals.

I once worked for a manager who, in some respects, may have been as intelligent and creative as anyone for whom I had ever worked. The problem with his style was that he would give us a skeleton of an idea and ask us to build upon it. When we sent it back, he would divulge a bit more of his plan and ask us for a revision. This would continue for weeks. The frustration we felt at having to work and rework his original product was enormous. Our discomfiture was only exacerbated when he took full credit for the work, expressing little or no gratitude to those of us who had "put the clothes on the mannequin." Employees get tired of a boss who continually changes the rules after the game has begun.

At its very core, the only difference between one organization and another is the performance of its employees. Managers love to talk about how the organization's most valuable asset is its people. Yet, when it comes to the proper care and maintenance of that valuable asset, I am reminded of the farmer who thought he could teach his mule to work without food. He complained later that, "...just about the time I had him trained, he up and died on me." If employees are continually held to impossibly high standards, treated like problems instead of people, and seldom given credit for their contributions, they will organizationally starve. The fool of a manager who casually says, "...if they don't like it, they can go somewhere else..." is thinking parochially and in a linear fashion. S/he is also predicting a bleak future.

Equally important is the assessment and assignment of blame. Inside an organization run by humans, mistakes are going to occur. They cannot be ignored or repeated with any degree of frequency without eventually causing considerable disruption to productivity. But there are some guidelines to follow when addressing negative employee behavior.

Initially, blame should not be assigned if it isn't deserved. I am continually amazed at the number of managers who feel obligated to "set the tone" when they take over a new work group. Assuming, without evidence, that everything was screwed up before s/he arrived on the scene is pompous and inaccurate. Problems may exist to be sure. But seldom is the case where a work area was in absolute disarray and in need of a complete overhaul.

Several years ago, my boss assigned me to take over a well-established work group that was made up of senior employees. They were well-intrenched into the administrative structure of the organization. He was unhappy with the performance of the group as a whole and was annoyed with all the internal bickering that appeared to be their most recognizable characteristic. He told me in no uncertain terms to "clean that mess up, and I don't care how many heads get lopped off in the process." I knew how to be a "change agent", and, although I did not relish the thought of using abrasive tactics, it certainly sounded like a  number of employees might need to be relocated before the process was complete. After three weeks in my new role, I began to suspect that things were not as bad as I had originally been led to believe. Although productivity was somewhat behind, it was not unreasonably so, and the members seemed to get along without near the reputed turmoil about which I had heard. The longer I watched, the better the work group looked. Two months into the assignment I reported to my boss that the problems he had articulated to me simply did not exist. In fact, I was rather enjoying the new experience which required less of my management time than my previous assignment had required.

"That's impossible," he sighed. "That group has been a rat's nest for the last year. They were so much trouble that the manager I replaced with you couldn't stand them."

Ahaaa!! Ahaaa!! Does or does not fish rot from the head? As it turned out, the members of the work group couldn't stand the manager either. One of the supervisors told me in confidence that the manager had advised them at the outset of his tenure that he trusted none of them…that trust was something they had to earn, and that he would insure that the people who screwed up would be held accountable. What an excellent way to get out of the blocks! Is it no surprise that once the manager departed, so did the productivity problems, the bickering , the trouble, and the turmoil. This is no commentary on **my** good management style. I really didn't do anything. But it is an indictment of **his** approach. Why shouldn't employees automatically have a manager's trust from the beginning? Any employee inclined to breach that trust will show his/her true colors before long anyway. Diplomacy is many times accomplished by thinking twice before saying nothing. Any thick-witted manager who seeks to establish a working foundation based on up-front and undeserved fear and intimidation is like the fool in the Bible who built his house upon the sand. In short term it will be washed away.

Finally, some discussion should be offered relative to who is to blame when things **do** go wrong, and how the situation should be handled. It is not required that managers absorb all the blame for the mistakes of their subordinates. Clearly, they should fix the blame appropriately, admonish inappropriate behavior, and take steps to prevent a repetition in the future.

Once again, this is more an argument about style rather than substance. Managers who berate, denounce, and damn the employee for doing something wrong have failed to realize that the employee is really an extension of him/herself...a resource which is incredibly valuable to accomplishing the mission. Carefully chosen words serve to focus on the problem rather than the person and permit a smoother transition back to work after the problem has been addressed. Too many managers use a battle-ax when a fly swatter is all that is needed. Does the "battle-ax" approach work? Sure, but is the result worth the concomitant damage? Hardly.

★ Managing to do it right...

1. Give credit and assign blame appropriately. The first should be done publicly, the second in private.
2. Be careful not to be so "result oriented" that you abuse subordinates in an effort to get the job done.
3. Give employees the benefit of the doubt. Trust them until they prove they cannot be trusted.
4. Admonish inappropriate behavior. It is your job to do so. But use only the amount of discipline necessary to achieve the desired result.
5. If things are not going well, look first to your management style. If some housekeeping is in order, clean your own house first.

CHAPTER FOUR

The Chicken Dance

"Caution: This cape does not enable user to fly."
Batman costume warning label.

Egomaniacs\e-go-ma'-ne-aks\n 1. Persons whose every conscious action is governed by their own self-interest. 2. Those who are self-obsessed to the point of illness. 3. At any given time, 5-10% of an organization's management team.

Perhaps you've heard of a song called "The Chicken Dance." It's a goofy little ditty which is played in beer halls and at dance festivals and goes...de-de-de-de-de-de-de de-de-de-de-de-de-de daa-daa-daa-daa daa-daa-daa-daa...to which people pop their fingers and opposable thumbs together to imitate chicken sounds, then strut around flapping their arms in time to the music, imitating a yard bird, and looking pretty much like a fool. Every time I witness this display, I am reminded of two things. One, how too much beer can increase the number of asinine things a prudent individual will do in public, and two, some of the managers I've known throughout my career.

A positive self-image is a good thing. I believe the good Lord meant for every human being to possess a healthy level of self-esteem and self-confidence. But for some reason, the promotion of certain people to a management position results in a gush of pomposity that causes them to do a never-ending chicken dance for anyone who will watch. In my younger years, I worked as a lifeguard at a municipal swimming pool. On busy days, for hours on end, all I would hear was the din of small children screaming, "Watch me, mommy...watch me, mommy...mommy, watch me...watch me, mommy." Then they would jump into the water with some twisted, contorted motion. What they were actually doing was of little importance as long as mommy was watching, and they were the center of attention. Unfortunately, many managers are the same way. Everything they do, every meeting they attend, even when they walk down the hall, their persona screams, "watch me…watch me…watch me…"

It gets tiresome for subordinates. The primary function of management is to remain outside the spotlight, facilitate the task, then bask in the afterglow which comes from giving the workers their chance to shine. But the "chicken dancers" can't stand it. Any opportunity to draw attention to themselves, to be the focus of attention, or to take credit is as addictive as cocaine to a drug abuser. Understand, now, that I am not talking about those managers who are natural leaders, gifted with a likeable personality, and infused with the charisma that automatically elevates them in the eyes of others. I'm talking about the managers who have few of those qualities and abuse their positions in order to feed their own egos. The techniques they use are numerous and varied. See if any of these exist in your organization:

Hyperbole—Chicken dancers are so self-focused that they can't talk about themselves or their accomplishments without amplifying, embellishing, magnifying, or enhancing the facts. In their defense, they don't even know they do it. They are so used to talking about how good they are, they can hardly wait to hear what they are going to say next. They are the Barney Fifes of the world. They can't help but talk it up, putting more spin on the yarn, and always making it bigger and better. The sad part about it is they don't fool anyone for very long. Even the most naïve listener begins after a while to question how any person can fly so high just because they walk around wearing a cape.

Despotism—The Bible speaks of Kings who would set upon their throne and permit or deny a person's access to them by raising or lowering their golden scepter. Anyone who sought an audience with such a king was required to wait at the entrance to the throne room until such time as the king raised the scepter. Absent such action by the king, presence before him was denied. Any violation resulted in dire circumstances for the violator. In keeping with that scriptural image, some managers view themselves not as managers, but as sovereigns of their own little kingdom.  They view their employees as peasants, and other managers as warring factions intent upon depriving them of their precious rule. They empower themselves by belittling those who work **for** them and bad mouthing those who work **with** them. They keep people waiting, interrupt during presentations, cut people off in mid-sentence, ask accusatory questions, and make impulsive decisions just because they can. These "little Hitlers" are consumed with a thirst for power. And yet they comprehend little about its use.

Falsification—This may seem like "hyperbole", but it is even more egregious. Some managers are simply liars. They either want to take credit, or want to avoid blame to such an extent that they will tell people whatever it takes to achieve that objective. This is an especially popular technique when subordinates need or want something which may prove difficult or distasteful for the manager to obtain. For example, to simply say that a subordinate's request was "denied" gets the manager off the hook, when, in fact, s/he never even tried to get it approved. But, the interesting thing about falsification is that it seldom works. Chicken dancers forget that the people who work for them are not stupid. They access other information sources, compare notes, talk to one another, and learn about the manager's reputation. Most times, however, they keep their suspicions to themselves, and so the guilty manager struts merrily along, proud and convinced that s/he got away clean with another lie.

Dodge Ball—I once worked along side a manager who was quite high up in the organization. To say I worked with him is to use the term loosely, because he didn't do a bit of work during the entire time, except to "dodge and dump." He was the most adept person I ever saw at sidestepping responsibility and evading work, while carrying the title of "executive manager." Every time our boss had a task for him to do, he was way too busy, had too many meetings, or was already swamped with makeshift responsibilities that seemed suspiciously unrecognizable to those of us who had to absorb his workload. It has been my experience that managers who either don't have what it takes to do their job, or simply don't **want** to do their job, busy themselves with petty activities that take up time, but accomplish little. If you notice this, beware. You have identified the "artful dodger."

Subjugation—The more people the chicken dancers have under their thumb, the happier they are. Although they want no responsibility of their own, they very much want a say so in everything everyone else does, including peers in other sections. They raise a ruckus about every decision made in which they had no input, even if it has no effect on their department. They fancy their role as that of a godfather whose ring must be kissed by anyone wanting to do anything inside the organization. They are empire builders who insist that subordinates be at their continual beck and call. They love to stifle projects by requesting additional useless research, re-submission, and re-approval. They insist that they be lobbied ahead of time for support and are especially pleased if begging is involved. They have an opinion on every subject regardless of their knowledge level and measure their power by the number of subordinates who appear tied to their apron strings. It is really rather nauseating to be around these peacocks.

Ajax the Lesser was a son of Oileus, King of Locris. He was one of the heroes in the Trojan War, but he had severe character flaws, such as being arrogant, boastful, and quarrelsome. He captured Cassandra, a daughter of King Priam, and raped her. He earned the enmity of his Greek allies because of this and left Troy to return home. His ship sunk in a storm, but he survived. He boasted long and loud about his escape, only to incur the wrath of Poseidon, who cast him back into the sea where he drowned.

Ajax was a charter member of the Chicken Dancer Club. Even so, Ajax had nothing on the chicken dancing managers of today. Most of them eventually get their just due, and their reputations hit the ground with a thud. But until that happens, they make a significant number of people miserable and negatively impact the organization as long as they are in charge. Ego is like salt. In small amounts, it can be effective and useful for enhancing flavor. Too much and the flavor is ruined…and like salt, once too much is added, it is difficult to remedy.

★   Managing to do it right…

1. Think about how others might view you before you initiate your management strut.
2. Tell it like it is. Exaggeration is very easy to recognize.
3. Managers manage. They do not rule. Organizations are not made up of individual empires to be ruled by zealots.
4. No manager's memory is good enough to lie on a regular basis.
5. Authority carries with it responsibility. Accept both or accept neither.
6. The nose is very near the mouth. If you enjoy leading people around by the nose, take care you do not get bit.

CHAPTER FIVE

A Vacuum Between The Ears

"In a hierarchy, employees tend to rise to their own level of incompetence." Lawrence Peter

Incompetence\(')in-'kom-pe-ten(t)s\n 1. Unsuitability for a particular purpose. 2. Lacking the intellectual qualities for effective action. 3. Possessing management mush for brains.

The Civil War battlefield leadership of Confederate General Braxton Bragg can best be described as a disastrous series of blunders and wasted opportunities. His conduct in battle camp was abysmal. His acerbic personality, reliance upon the power of his rank, strict discipline policies, and mediocre intellect caused him to be thoroughly detested by most of the officers and men under his command. When General Nathan Bedford Forrest could stand the incompetence no longer, he addressed Bragg as follows: "I have stood your incompetence for as long as I intend to. You have played the part of a damned scoundrel, you are a coward, and if you were any part of a man I would slap your jaws and force you to resent it. You may as well not issue further orders to me, for I will not obey them. I will hold you personally responsible for any further indignities you endeavor to inflict upon me…and I say to you that if you ever again try to interfere with me or cross my path, it will be at the peril of your life."

Pretty stern words for a subordinate to wage at his superior. And yet, there is probably not a subordinate alive who, at one time or another, hasn't yearned for the opportunity to scream similarly at his/her boss, especially if the boss frequently displays signs of incompetence. If life were fair, there would be a truckload of managers who, rather than holding management positions would be making their living by asking, "Do you want fries with that?" But life is not fair. Some managers don't know chicken poop from chicken salad, yet they hold positions of authority and make management decisions that contain more holes than a piece of swiss cheese.

Incompetence is a dangerous thing because it is an unconscious/conscious type of existence. Although intelligence appears to be missing, the desire for authority is not. One thing the incompetent manager is aware of is that s/he possesses organizational power. S/he learns very quickly that where talent is absent, power can suffice if the manager is threatened or intimidated. Subordinates rarely take on an incompetent boss as Forrest did Bragg. The reason is obvious. They need their job, and making an enemy of the boss is a good way to lose it. Instead, they worry, cry, yell at their spouses, kick the dog, and within the safety of their peers poke fun at the boss, call him/her names, and hope s/he derails at some point in the near future. But it can be a miserable, lonely existence for a subordinate who yearns to be productive and get things done, but is caught in a strangle hold by an unqualified and incapable domnoddy.

Incompetent managers rely heavily on rules, policies, and procedures. They seldom engage in, or allow work activities which might be construed as creative, innovative, or on the edge. They find safety in the regulations, and automatically look for reasons to say, "no." They are also very discipline-oriented. If you whip a dog enough times, the dog ceases to do anything except cower. Cowering employees may not accomplish much, but they don't engage in activities which might threaten an incompetent manager's security.

The frustration experienced by subordinates is exacerbated when they seek to do the incompetent boss's bidding based upon unclear and incomplete direction. Incompetent managers seldom know what they want. As a result, their instructions are frequently distorted and confusing. I was once told by my boss to "make a list of all the unknown problems I expected to encounter in the new project we were starting." How dumb is that? But knowing him the way I did, I knew that arguing would get me nowhere. So I created a list and facetiously entitled it *Unknown Problems Which We Have Identified*. He reviewed it, approved it, and tacked it on his bulletin board where it stayed for the remainder of the project.

An incompetent manager will seldom answer questions directly and immediately. Whenever subordinates go into his/her office, the manager will be holding papers which indicate s/he is in the middle of something important which requires his/her full and immediate attention. Employees shouldn't be surprised if the manager asks that questions be submitted in written form. This requires time on the subordinate's part and delays the need for immediate action from the manager. Further, it will probably get lost.  Incompetent managers stack reams of paper in and around their office. To the casual observer, last month's work looks just like this month's work, so it's difficult to tell exactly how busy the manager really is.

Incompetent managers will seldom delegate responsibility. That would require that they monitor the work activity and stay one step ahead of those doing the work. To the incompetent boss, slow movement is good. Status quo is better. If s/he does delegate work, s/he usually gives insufficient instructions then disappears with no forwarding address. Employees must then either wait for additional guidance or guess at what the manager actually wanted. And don't bother leaving messages either. During one project, our manager told us not to leave him voicemails regarding our projects because they took up too much message room on his machine. Duh! What's the machine for anyway? He said he preferred to address project issues personally. The problem was he was never anywhere to be found.

The final scary reality about incompetent managers is that they find safety in numbers. They actively seek out other incompetents and team up to feed off of each other. Where one incompetent manager may feel intimidated, two or more find solace by convincing one another that their management approach is not only correct, but healthy for the organization. We used to hate it when our incompetent boss had lunch with one of his incompetent buddies. He always came back full of himself and armed with more busy work ideas for us. Incompetence and arrogance make for a revolting combination.

Fortunately, most of the managers in an organization are not totally and completely incompetent. However, all of us, regardless of our position, are ignorant of some things. Throughout my public safety management career, I was transferred over a dozen times, most times to a section or division with which I was unfamiliar. Although it made me a well-rounded manager in the long run, there existed periods of time where I was totally dependent upon the people who worked for me to bring me up to speed relative to the specific job function I was managing. In nearly every case, my subordinates were willing to assist me, as long as I was willing to admit that I didn't know everything and needed their help.

Managers who assume they possess absolute knowledge just because they are in charge are numskulls. It isn't always necessary to totally re-engineer a work group just to prove you can. I would be willing to bet that General Forrest would have had much to offer General Bragg had Bragg been smart enough to know that he didn't know it all.

★ Managing to do it right…

1. Be willing to admit that you as a manager have both strengths and weaknesses. Build on your strengths and take steps to identify and compensate for your weak points.
2. A healthy sense of self-esteem is a good thing. Arrogance and haughtiness are not. Take measures to see that you do not assume a "holier than thou" posture.
3. If you don't know what you are doing, don't start changing things. Not only are you interfering, you might be causing tremendous damage.
4. If you possess a severe management deficiency, get some help. There is hardly any missing link which cannot be bridged with the proper training and/or mentoring support.

CHAPTER SIX

My Final Decision Is Not To Decide. Unless, Of Course, I Decide Differently

"*I have opinions of my own—strong opinions. But I don't always agree with them.*" Former President George Bush

Decisiveness\di-`si-siv-nis\n 1. Having the power and ability to make sound and resolute decisions. 2. A concept about which many managers are undecided.

Managers have many duties and responsibilities in addition to decision-making. But all managers must make decisions. It is integral to their position, and they are expected to do so on a frequent basis. It is interesting (and would be humorous were it not so prolific) to examine the methods used by certain managers to determine everything from who makes the coffee to how millions of dollars get spent. Managers, just like subordinates, have opinions—strong ones. But some managers, unlike former President Bush, not only agree with their own opinions, but have little or no room for anyone else's ideas. In looking at the ways managers make decisions (or fail to make them), I have identified five different decision-making arenas: Refutation, constraint, authority, compromise, and consensus.

Refutation: Simply ignore the problem, and it will go away. This is the technique of choice for the weak, untrained procrastinator who is so concerned with **keeping** his/her job that s/he avoids **doing** the job. Not that refusing to make a decision is always wrong. If there exists no reason to make a decision in the first place, or if making a decision results in the deterioration of a situation, then avoiding a decision may be prudent. However, such is seldom the case. Managers who seek to avoid decision-making, yet know they cannot simply ignore the problem, will engage their dilemma by doing two things. First, they will create a committee to study the problem. They will define the problem to the group, and insist that, somewhere down the road, the group return with a single alternative or solution about which they are all in agreement. Secondly, the manager will become intricately involved in a multitude of minor, inconsequential, day-to-day tasks which are, for all intents and purposes, meaningless to the overall forward movement of the organization. Managers, as a rule, make too many small decisions which should be delegated anyway. But the refutation manager takes this activity to the level of an art form. In so doing, this manager is convinced that people around him/her will be impressed at how really busy s/he is, while, at the same time, delaying action on any committee recommendations. Even if the committee returns with a single decision recommendation, the manager, by virtue of being so busy, can delay action indefinitely. This is a cowardly way to approach decision-making and impresses no one.

Constraint. Constraint is a suppressive approach to decision-making which places more emphasis on the people involved in the decision-making process than it does on the decision itself. Depending upon the circumstances, this may not necessarily be bad. Some years back, my manager was able to secure a much-improved work area for us, complete with new equipment and increased storage space. Although we were eager to take ownership of the new "digs," we were less than enamoured with her decision that all moving would have to be accomplished on Saturday and Sunday, our regular days off. Further, we were somewhat put off that we had not been consulted on a decision which directly affected our non-working time. We could have refused. We could also have filed a grievance with the union. But the bottom line was that our manager was a good boss, with a good heart, who seldom asked anything of us that was unreasonable or unfair. Because our relationship with her was more important than the decision to fight moving on a weekend, we took a more constrained approach and went along with her announced intentions. When a decision is not especially critical, and the relationship with the people involved in the process is, in fact, more important than the decision itself, constraint can prove valuable.

Unfortunately, many managers, even good managers, believe that no decision is worth engendering conflict. I disagree. Most decisions are neither totally right nor totally wrong. More accurately, they are hybrids which are more good than bad and result from the hashing and rehashing of contrasting opinions and conflicting alternatives. Ideas which have been through the fire of presentation, rebuttal, defense, and discussion, are more clear, more easily articulated, and more ready for immediate action. In normal situations, this type of process is accompanied by conflict and contention. Disagreements develop and tempers may flair. At times, the competition for ideas gets out of balance with team member coordination. It takes energy on the manager's part to referee such conflicts, and, if necessary, reject subordinate suggestions

while still
protecting
the feelings
of the partic-
ipants. Still
in all, to
avoid such a
process

because it may be uncomfortable is irresponsible decision-making. It is incumbent upon the senior manager to remind everyone involved that when the dogfight is over, everyone is still on the same team and working toward the same goals. Although it is no secret that fools and dissidents will seek to derail this process, their individual agendas must be ignored, and the emphasis must remain on working together to hammer out the appropriate solution to the problem.

Power. Power has its place in the decision-making process too. When a police officer walks into a bar fight, s/he can't just say, "I'll tell you what. I'm gonna collect a little data here, go back to police headquarters, consider some alternatives, and return with a decision later." No. The time for a decision is right then, before anyone else gets hurt, or more property gets destroyed. By the same token, Army generals do not gain their reputations as leaders by facilitating consensus decision-making sessions during times of battle. They make decisions, bark out orders, and expect them to be followed without question. Power does, in fact, have its place.

But organizations are neither bar fights nor battlefields. In fact, the managers who most frequently resort to power when making organizational decisions would probably not be effective as leaders during times of crisis. Decision power-mongers rely almost solely on their position as evidence of their expertise. They are intimidated by face to face competition, especially as it relates to decisions they are charged to make. In many cases, they have closed minds and inflexible, preconceived notions which lead to shallow, indefensible decisions. They start out with a conclusion, then go about looking for facts to support it. Although they may pretend to seek input from others, all they really want is support for their convoluted ideas and respect for their rank. They are not interested in any alternative which threatens their own. Their skin is paper thin because, although they would never admit it, they have absolutely no business being in a management position, and have neither the talent nor the disposition to accept that someone else might have a better idea of how to get things done. Many times they have their own agendas which are not just out in left field, they aren't even in the ball park. If I seem particularly harsh on this group, it's because they are dangerous to the organization in general and to the innocent subordinates who are honestly trying to do a good job and assist management by providing their best ideas.

What is especially nauseating about the power-based decision-makers is their desire to be a screener of everyone else's decisions. Section managers, who are mocked for their own silly personnel decisions, get insulted if they are not allowed to participate in the personnel decisions of sections which are none of their business. Division leaders, who procrastinate on operational plans and organizational strategies of their own, constantly throw up road blocks to other managers who are actually getting the work done. And financial administrators, whose job it is to simply approve funds and reallocate money, try to play the role of budget czar by deciding who gets how much and when. These power-crazed fanatics, as Lawrence Peter so aptly put it, have been promoted above their level of competence. It is amazing that so many of them reach this point. Even more saddening is that they are like athlete's foot, they never, ever go away. They are bulls in the organizational china shop who consistently do more damage than good.

Compromise. Depending upon with whom you talk, compromise may or may not be an effective decision-making technique. To a dirty camper in the winter woods, an icy cold bath in a spring might be better than no bath at all, but from the story in the Biblical book of Solomon, a half-baby is clearly **not** a better decision than no baby at all. In a compromise, no one really gets what s/he wants. Everyone simply continues to give a little until they meet somewhere in the middle. What the final product becomes, as well as the time required for its creation, is important. If the final decision is so watered down that it becomes too weak a medicine to effectively treat the disease, it is a mistake. Also, if the compromise process takes so long that the eventual decision becomes obsolete before it can be implemented, this too becomes a decision-making failure. Compromise too often becomes the manager's response to pessimists and nay-sayers in the group. Many times these employees generate questions which force the decision-maker to weigh the risks and disadvantages of a particular decision. But eventually, the manager must force a commitment from them. To water down a decision just to shut them up is a cop-out.

Consensus. Consensus decision-making, on its face, seems admirable. The manager who can lead a team to arrive at an agreeable solution is usually perceived as charismatic and successful. Consensus is generally preferable to conflict—but not always. The manager who seeks consensus at all costs, or refuses to act in the face of subordinate disagreement has stepped into quicksand. S/he is in danger of falling victim to the "groupthink" phenomenon. Groupthink is an important, negative experience that arises in group decision-making which can result in disastrous consequences. Groupthink is the tendency of a group to strive for solidarity and unanimity so strongly that members will avoid being critical, asking questions, or engaging in disputes which are required to arrive at a good decision. During Groupthink, in-group pressures are so intense, that members will suppress their desire to express different perspectives. In some circumstances, members who question group views, or express a different perspective will be humiliated, embarrassed, disciplined, or even dismissed from the group. Groupthink leads a group to believe that it has achieved consensus when, in fact, the group has not engaged in critical analysis at all. Very simply, too much harmony and conformity with groups can cause Groupthink at the expense of critical thinking. Unrealistic and ill-considered decisions are made during Groupthink processes. Managers who are so concerned with consensus that they lose their decision-making focus will seldom reach a reliable and applicable solution.

★ Managing to do it right…

1. Management decision-making is a complex task which must be learned if a manager is to be successful.
2. The manager who can work with others to frame intelligent questions with regard to organizational decisions is far more success-prone than the one who claims to have **all** of the answers.
3. Ignoring decisions which need to be made will seldom make them go away.
4. Management decisions are not always totally right or totally wrong. The goal is to develop a good decision-making batting average that contributes to the organization's overall mission.
5. Refutation, constraint, power, compromise, and consensus can be effective and/or ineffective decision-making processes depending on how and when they are used by the manager.

CHAPTER SEVEN

Round and Round and Round It Goes. Where It Stops, Nobody Knows

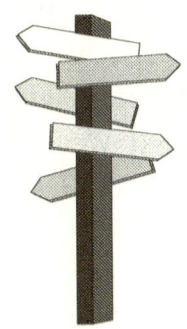

Alice: "Would you please tell me which way I ought to go from here?"

Cheshire Cat: "Well, that depends a good deal on where you want to go."

Alice: "...I don't much care where..."

Cheshire Cat: Then it doesn't much matter which way you go."

Alice: "...So long as I get <u>somewhere</u>."

Cheshire Cat: Oh, you're sure to do that, if only you walk long enough."

Alice in Wonderland; Through the Magic Looking Glass

Whirligig\wher-li-gig\n 1. A child's toy which, when spun, whirls around in a circle, eventually coming to rest in the same place. 2. A manager with no vision or direction.

John F. Kennedy didn't know the first thing about space travel. He had no educational background in aeronautical engineering and couldn't read a schematic. He did, however, have a vision. As President of the United States, he saw America as the leader in space exploration. He believed it could be done and articulated the vision with such fervor that the entire country believed we could do it. And we did. Therein lies the importance of management vision. Whenever something significant is accomplished, its origin can be traced not back to a manager who goes around in circles, but to a manager who had a vision and set a definite direction for his/her subordinates.

Managers who have no vision may work hard, but they don't accomplish much. Sadly, managers who only look one week ahead are, in some respects, more popular because they fit in well with the rest of the reactionary crowd. Managers without vision look at a rock pile and see it as an obstacle which must be cleared. The manager with vision looks at the same rock pile and imagines a cathedral. Some managers are naturally better at visioning than others—but visions must be developed if an organization seeks stability and desires high levels of productivity.

Vision is not a popular subject with run-of–the-mill managers. Primarily because it involves thinking, and thinking outside the box at that! It is so much easier to do things the same way day after day, year after year. I once worked for a manager who periodically went through the motions of asking his subordinates for new ideas. But whenever someone offered one, his response was usually something like, "Good. Please research this completely and present me with a detailed progress report of your findings." After a couple of these punishing assignments, we subordinates learned to keep our mouths shut and our ideas to ourselves. No sense suggesting something new if you're just going to get administratively spanked for your trouble. And that's the way it is so much of the time. Regardless of the lip service, many managers don't want to be troubled with ethereal rhetoric about vision and direction. Managers with no long-range vision soon fill their agendas with routine, reactive, non-productive activities.

Therefore, when you bring up the subject of management vision, you will encounter a bellyful of excuses from management hamsters who are perfectly willing to climb daily into their wheel and engage in repetitious process-oriented activities. The following are some of the more frequent excuses for avoiding visionary management:

1. **All the creative stuff has already been done. There's nothing new under the sun.** Truth be known, most visions are not really new visions. They are modifications, mutations, revisions, and/or restatements of older visions which are successful elsewhere. Visioning need not necessarily be the equivalent of the Biblical creation. But it can really help to address philosophies, dreams, ideals, and plans for the future. The best managers are always re-evaluating work

methods to see if there might not be a better way of doing things. Lightweight managers avoid such activities because they require energy. It's always easier to keep doing stuff in the same old way, but its not always best.

2. **I'm not the top manager in the organization, therefore, it's not my job.** "It's not my job" is the mantra of the management sloth. Certainly, an organizational vision must be articulated by top management. But just because you're not the lead dog on the sled team is no reason to shirk your responsibility to run. The development and implementation of goals, objectives, and procedures which support the overall organizational direction is the middle manager's explicit responsibility. Successful visions, once they are initially developed, must be lived and executed in details, not broad-brush strokes. It is every manager's responsibility to "get into the ball game." Last time I checked, managing was not a spectator sport.

3. **What difference does it make? Organizational change interferes with it anyway.** What a ridiculous statement. A well-developed vision is not threatened by organizational change. It is, in fact, the very antithesis of instability. An inspiring vision serves as a compass in a stormy sea. It is flexible enough to be adjusted but finely tuned and stable enough to reveal direction accurately.

4. **It's just the same old stuff wrapped in a new package.** Maybe so. But that doesn't diminish its effectiveness. Some years back, the American interest in wine exploded. With it, the wine growing regions of the United States began to produce higher quantities and qualities of wine for American consumption. A wine company which, up to that time, had experienced insignificant competition began to see its market share drop considerably. In examining their wine production processes, the company realized that, although the wine itself was a good product, it was still being bottled in the same dreary brown bottle, with the same tired looking label they had always used. In an effort to improve their image, management changed from the dark brown frumpy bottle to a new sleek golden bottle. They also designed a fresh, new label which portrayed a new image of vitality and vigor. They made no changes to the wine itself. Within the first six months of the new issue, they reclaimed 27% of their market share. The idea worked—same wine, new bottle. Sometimes a fresh package is all that is needed to get things rolling again.

5. **My company doesn't produce a product, so vision really isn't necessary.** Well, if that's true, why do literally millions of parents spend exorbitant amounts of money to send their children to private schools instead of using the tax-based public school system? Organizations that provide a service require vision as much or maybe even more than product-producing companies. Customers of service-based providers do not have a trinket or toy to hold in their

hand as a result of their interaction. Consequently, the level of service they encounter, and the speed, efficiency, and courtesy with which they are treated, becomes increasingly important. Any company who treats these important customer needs with an impulsive, cavalier approach is asking for trouble.

6. **It doesn't matter whether we are visionary or not. We're the only game in town.** Spoken like a true bureaucrat. If government were profit-based, it would be bankrupt by the middle of next week. It is true that citizens have little choice relative to the governmental services they receive. They can't simply go out and get another police department or fire department just because they are unhappy with the present level of service they receive. Given that, the onus is always on the public service entities to constantly seek better ways to serve the people who contribute to their financial support.

Developing an organizational vision is a management responsibility. It is one of the factors that separates managers from supervisors. It makes absolutely no sense to begin a road trip without deciding ahead of time where you are going and having some idea of how to get there. Direction doesn't happen arbitrarily. It is developed. It doesn't matter that the newly created vision more closely resembles a marsupial than a perfectly formed infant. It sometimes takes time for the vision to assume meaningful color and form. What is important is that the manager invest the time and energy to create it. A refusal to do so makes him/her no more productive than the whirligig which works very hard going around in circles then eventually stops having never moved from where it started.

★   Managing to do it right...

1. Realize that the development of direction and vision makes you an "accomplishment" oriented manager rather than just an "activity" oriented one.
2. Build in time to think and be creative. Without an assertive attempt to do this, you will become bogged down with the reactionary process of dealing with day-to-day problems.
3. Ask questions and seek information from all levels of the organization. Employees stand ready to assist you if you will include them in your visionary research process.
4. Review and discard all of the excuses for avoiding the visioning process.
5. Accept the development of a vision as a primary responsibility of your management position. There is no reason for not doing so.

CHAPTER EIGHT

Don't Just Sit There, Do Something!

"If You Ain't Laying Any Eggs, It's Time To Get Out Of The Henhouse." C. David Smith

**Production\pro-duk-shen\n 1. The   creation   of
something useful. 2. The total output of an organization or industry. 3. Third year Hebrew to some managers.**

I have had the distinct pleasure of working for some wonderful managers throughout my career. One of the best is my
present boss who manages in the educational organization
that pays my salary. Once in a while, he will stroll through the
office complex, sometimes on a Friday afternoon, and ask
me, "Are you laying any eggs?" If I admit to loafing a bit, he'll
sometimes retort, "Well, if you ain't laying any eggs, then its
time to get out of the henhouse."

One of the important leadership principles that he understands well is that employees are not going to push wheelbar-
rows one hundred percent of the time. But instead of
stomping his feet and pounding the desk, he turns it into a
positive experience, sending us home a little early and rein-
forcing our mindset that when we get back to the nest, we'll
lay eggs that much harder.

In the last chapter, we discussed the need for a manager to
have a well thought-out vision of what needs to be accomplished. But that is only half of the story. The next step is for
the manager to translate that vision to his/her subordinates
and lead them to accomplish something meaningful. In other
words, you've got to **do** something. You've got to be productive. You've got to make something concrete out of the vision
or it deteriorates into nothing more than a pipe dream.

Too many managers, especially new ones, are so concerned
about doing something wrong that they prefer to do nothing

for a time. Unfortunately this mindset can become habit forming. True, very few mistakes are made if nothing is being done, but that's not why organizations exist. A sailboat is much safer in the harbor than it is upon the seas, but sailboats are not made to sit around in the harbor.

We once inherited a boss who explained to us, his new subordinates, at our first staff meeting, that **his** success as a manager was founded upon what he called his "middle of the stream" approach. He wanted us to think of our group as one canoe in a stream with lots of other organizational canoes. As long as we kept our canoe right in the middle, out of everyone else's way, we would all move along just fine. No paddling faster than the others, no paddling slower than the others, no calling attention to us as different, no rocking the boat. He called it "organizational blending."

And you know what? It worked. Because we were employed in a tax-supported service industry, there was really no need to produce. We just floated along, doing nothing, collecting our paychecks, and passing time. The problem with this non-confrontational approach is that it equates to lazy management. It creates complacent employees, rewards inactivity, and gets nothing accomplished.

Some managers are not quite as blatant as my "middle of the stream" example. They manage to exert the same effect, but they do it with a "what if?" approach. What if this idea causes a cost overrun? What if this idea has already been tried with negative results? What if upper management refuses to back us? The truth is if a frog had wings, it wouldn't bump its butt every time it moved. But that doesn't stop the frog from going where he wants and needs to go. Management is not the art of preventing things from going wrong. It is not defined as routine maintenance, or being satisfied that the organization is doing an average job. Managers who think that way are setting the organization on a direct course for mediocrity.

I alluded to this in an earlier chapter, but it bears further emphasis. Things may stay the same for a long time, but it should not be because management has not examined them, tested them, analyzed them, and attempted to find more effective and efficient ways of doing them. Production is an evolving concept. Certainly it begins with a vision. But it cannot stop there.

I can't tell you how many work teams of which I've been a member where we studied a proposal, considered its risk, decided it was worth trying, even targeted an inception date, but never got off the dime and implemented it. Why? Because somebody wanted to study it further, or was afraid it might not work, or was worried that others might not hop on the wagon and support the project. The bottom line is that fear of failure equates to a failure to **do**! Every sports coach in the nation will tell you that going into a game with the mindset of "not losing" as opposed to "doing everything it takes to win" is counter productive. A famous football coach once addressed his team at the beginning of the season and said,

"Men, I want you to think of one word all season. One word and one word only 'Super Bowl'" (two words). Although his word count was off, his heart was in the right place.

Too many managers successfully define their legacy as an extended period where they were in charge, and nothing went wrong. How sad. A poet (me) who perhaps understands more about management than he does about poetry once penned a poem. It goes like this:

"The Importance of Maintaining a Positive Attitude, Even When You Don't Know How to Proceed, By Faking It Until You Figure It Out"

If you can…
Do.
If you can't…
You
Must learn enough…
To Bluff
Stuff,
Long enough
To think things
through
So you can
Eventually
Do.

The poem begins with "doing", and it ends with "doing." It never considers "not doing" as an option.

Sometimes the only time I get to exercise is late in the evening. One night recently I was jogging around my neighborhood at about 11:00 p.m. I was just about done, having completed my three miles, and was looking forward to the end. Several blocks from home, I realized that my shoe was untied. I stopped, bent over, and spent a few seconds to retie it. When I looked up from my awkward and still kneeling position, it was perilously obvious that my situation had changed. I was now looking right down the muzzle of the biggest, blackest Doberman Pinscher I had ever seen. His nose was so close to mine that I could feel the breath from his nostrils. I have seldom found myself in a position where I absolutely, positively did not know what to do. But as I stared at him, and he stared at me, I had the strong suspicion that this stalemate would not be indefinite. So I did the only thing my terrified mind could conjure up at that second. I looked him right in the eye and as politely as I could, I whispered, "How ya doin'?" He didn't move a muscle. He just stared. After what must only have been a few seconds (although it felt like time was standing still) I heard a female voice call, "Bobo! Come here, Bobo!" The dog flinched his head the slightest bit in the direction of the voice. Since he had blinked first, I felt a tiny bit more confident. So, still not moving, I said to the dog, "Bobo? Bobo's a sissy name." His tail wagged one time. By then his owner was close enough to say, "Oh, he won't hurt you. He's just a big pussy cat." After she hooked him onto his leash, I defiantly petted his head and cautiously continued my wobbly-legged journey home. By the time I arrived, I had a story replete with details about how I'd stared down this mammoth of a dog, called him a sissy, and was none the worse for it. But I've got to admit that for just a second, I was, as the poem says, looking for a way to bluff until I could come up with a plan that might save my bacon.

The story is true, and a little silly, but it makes a good point. Not every challenge a manager runs up against is going to be accompanied by an easy solution. To further complicate things, the decision s/he makes may turn out to be critical. But the effective manager must take the initiative to "stare the dog down" as it were, regardless of the outcome. Managers have to get things done. They must make things happen. Their posture must be offensive and production-oriented. Their reluctance to do so injures their reputation, discourages subordinates, and is a complete disservice to the organization.

★ Managing to do it right...

1. If you are managing good, productive employees who support your goals and work hard, praise them and occasionally give them a break.
2. Understand that ideas and visions are an important first step. The second step is to bring those ideas to fruition.
3. Don't try to blend into the background. If that theory worked, vanilla would be the only ice cream flavor in existence.
4. Don't be afraid of failure. Try it. If it doesn't work, can it and try something else.
5. Measure your management success by how many things you get done, not by how few things go wrong.
6. If you run into a Doberman late at night, just hope his name is Bobo.

CHAPTER NINE

Behold The Jackass—How It Brays

"No one will believe you solved this problem so quickly. We've been working on it for months. Now, go act busy for a few more weeks, and I'll let you know when it's time to tell them." Senior Executive, Solar Systems, Inc. (to a subordinate)

Jackass\'jak-ass\n 1. Donkey, esp; a male donkey. 2. A stubborn, stupid management misfit.

In the movie "Patton", George C. Scott, in a fit of rage, pulled out his pistol, shot two jackasses, and ordered them thrown over a bridge because they were stalling the progress of one of his troop movements. His actions shocked the soldiers who witnessed them and thoroughly traumatized the animals' owner. There is little question that he effectively removed the obstacle, but his methodology smacked of killing a mosquito with a claw hammer.

You won't be in the workplace for very long before you discover that there's a jackass parked on many of the organizational bridges you attempt to cross. And if you choose to use a pistol to dispatch each jackass, you'll run out of bullets long before the job is done. Too bad that so many of these long-eared mokes turn out to be in charge. With managers of this ilk, it is almost a given that "stubbornness" accompanies "stupidity." If stupid managers **realized** that they were stupid and would simply get out of the way, things could still get accomplished. But Noooooooooo! They plant themselves clearly in the way. Then, either intentionally or unintentionally, interfere with every positive work action they see. The major problem with these managers (hang with me here) is that they don't know what they're doing, but they don't **know** that they don't know. If they **knew** that they didn't know, they wouldn't be nearly so dangerous because, although they would be of no help, they might know enough to stay out of the way.

I once had the miserable misfortune to work with one of these yokels during my later practitioner years. Fortunately, we were organizational peers and, although I had to work **with** him, I did not have to work **for** him. This manager saw it as his role (and it became his passion) to slow the progress of almost every project (except his own) by smothering its advocates with question after question during endless and unproductive meetings. Whenever you heard him say, "I just have a few questions for you..." you knew that the donkey was now cooling his heels smack in the middle of the bridge, and that all movement was coming to a disconcerting halt. Most of the time, the questions were poorly asked, dealt with information which had already been provided in written form, or focused on unknown factors which could be answered only as the project moved forward. The frustration and delay he generated was enormous. And I would dare say a number of solid ideas were stifled even before they came to him because employees were unwilling to endure his eminent but pointless interrogations.

Now, I don't mean to suggest that we charge forward with every proposal *sans* enough meaningful dialogue and sufficient information to reduce the risk as much as possible. But once that has been accomplished, getting on with the work must become the priority.

Some managers simply fail to employ the concept of "reasonableness." If it is **reasonable** to deal with a problem, and if the alternatives to solving it appear **reasonable**, and if a **reasonable** approach is supported by **reasonable** people, then the manager needs to stop stalling and move the work team toward a solution. The manager's job is to look for ways to dodge obstacles, not to become one. Most times, people understand the goal. The conflict revolves around the means by which the goal is to be achieved. Reasonable managers know that the cat can be skinned a number of different ways. If you are the boss, it might be necessary, in the interest of efficiency, to acquiesce to the ideas of others, even though they may differ from your own. The manager who can do this accomplishes two things. First of all, the problem gets solved, and secondly, the manager comes across as a flexible leader rather than a dictator.

Next, managers must work to prevent becoming an inadvertent bottleneck. Bottleneckers allow everything from routine paperwork to fast-tracked projects to land and lay on their desk for unacceptable lengths of time. The manager who sets due dates for everyone under his/her control, then allows finished products to sit around without some type of timely action sends the message that s/he cares little about getting things done.

Another problem is the management practice of "analysis paralysis." This is simply studying a problem to death, without ever taking action on the pertinent issues. Clearly it is the job of management to insure that all efforts inside the organization proceed on a timely, efficient path toward the accomplishment of the goals which have been established. But that requires some type of **movement**. Active problem-solving demands the development and assessment of alternatives to be sure. But once those alternatives have been evaluated and narrowed, the time comes to make some decisions and follow through. The arduous process of analyzing from every possible perspective, then going back to the drawing board, then studying it some more from yet another direction smacks of the would-be author who never gets anything written because s/he constantly keeps going back to edit that which is already done. In fact, managers who engage in analysis paralysis are simply practicing decision-avoidance. Effective managers evaluate alternatives, make decisions, solve problems, and move on. The jackass, on the other hand, simply sits and brays. Such a practice makes a lot of noise, but accomplishes little.

★   Managing to do it right...

1. Remember that your job as a manager is to guide and energize. Keep your people moving toward the goal.
2. Employ reasonable solutions to solve reasonable problems. Don't overreact.
3. Insure that you are not blocking the bridge. Let your employees think and work. Ask intelligent questions, but avoid analysis paralysis.
4. Let your actions speak for you, lest you be accused of braying.

CHAPTER TEN

I Don't Play Politics—I Work At It

"In the political arena, some days you are the bug, and some days you are the windshield." Anonymous

Snake\'snak\n 1. A scaled reptile with a long tapering body. 2. A worthless, treacherous person. 3. Managers who slither throughout the organization seeking prey.

You've probably heard the old saying that politicians and diapers have one thing in common. They should both be changed regularly and for the same reason. Unfortunately, most organizations are riddled with organizational politicians who actually bloom and grow at the management level. In our supervision and management classes we give the students a political action survey which is designed to identify their individual tendencies toward craving power and playing politics. True to form, we discover in almost every instance that the comfort with, and desire for political involvement increases in the management ranks.

Almost any place you find politics, you will find a degree of abuse. Usually it is in the form of inconsistency. It is one of the major battles fought among managers, and it can get particularly nasty when it deals with dress codes, evaluation methods, pay scales, benefits, and work rules. These benchmarks serve as the standards by which "fairness" is determined, and the emotions that surround them can generate arguments, hard feelings, and accusations of partiality.

It is almost inconceivable that some managers willingly, even enthusiastically embrace the inappropriate incongruities with which subordinates are treated. The same manager who will transfer someone within his/her workgroup without a word to his peers, will scream bloody murder if another manager in another workgroup does the same without his/her endorsement.

It is imperative that managers strive for consistency in the decisions they make and in the way they communicate their decisions to others. To do otherwise can be politically destructive, even if the manager's heart is in the right place. The story of David and Bob proves my point well.

Several years ago, one of our managers, David, was appointed as Chief Executive Officer of our company. David was notified on Thursday morning, and his promotion was to become effective the next Monday. David's first action was to go and see his good friend, Bob. He told Bob that, "On Monday, I'm going to promote you and make you a member of my staff." Bob was elated. It was a job he had wanted for years, and, although David had told him to "keep it quiet" until Monday, Bob couldn't help but call his wife and parents to give them the good news. Later on Friday, David attended the executive staff meeting where he was congratulated by members of his support staff. When the excitement died down, David began by saying, "As you all know, one of my first jobs on Monday will be to make a promotion. I would be interested in your opinions as a staff on whom that person should be." As they went around the table, David sat stunned as he listened to their feedback. To the person, they stated that they could work with anyone he selected with the exception of Bob. They cited Bob's lack of experience, argumentative nature, and his unwillingness to work as a team player. David left the meeting feeling sick to his stomach. He had not even received his appointment, and he was already embroiled in his first political conflict. If he promoted Bob, he would be sending a message to his staff that he had no confidence in their decision-making ability. On the other hand, how could he go back to his good friend and tell him he had changed his mind? Needless to say, it was a sleepless weekend.

Before I tell you how the story ends, let's look at the political mistakes committed by this manager. Initially, he should never have shown his cards until the game actually began. Too many times, managers, in the excitement of the moment, promise things to others which turn out to be difficult to deliver. Mark my word, if you start making concrete plans for your eggs before they are completely in your basket, you're libel to end up with yoke all over your face. Secondly, he made a decision to promote Bob, and simply couldn't wait to tell him. Then he went to his staff secretly seeking their tacit approval of Bob, rather than demonstratively announcing his  decision to them. And it backfired. One of the major differences between a shark and a jellyfish is the presence of a spine. If you really want the opinion of others, ask for it with an open mind and no preconceived notions. On the other hand, if you make a decision, have the political wherewithal to confidently announce your decision and stand by it.

On Monday, David went to Bob's office. Behind closed doors, an embarrassed, chagrined C.E.O. advised Bob that he would not be getting the promotion. It was a humiliating experience that never needed to happen. The real shame of the story was that Bob probably **was** the best choice for the promotion, but David could not go back to his staff endorsing Bob because of the political boner he had pulled with them on Friday.

Playing political games with others is a dangerous proposition. At the least, it makes people angry, and at the most it can be emotionally and professionally devastating.

As a young, trusting police manager, I was called into the Chief's office one day. I was told that a major golf tournament involving local judges, attorneys, politicians, etc. was to be held in the near future. Our vice unit had good information that significant gambling was involved. They intended to bust the tournament and secure the arrest of all those involved who were gambling illegally. In that I had a brother who ran a local golf course, the chief and deputy chief wanted to know if my brother might have access to the player roster, and whether he would be willing to secretly supply the police department with such a list. I called my brother and asked. He procured the player roster, and I went to his golf course to pick it up. I asked if he were playing in the tournament. He replied that he had been asked, but was still unsure. I informed him to stay away as police action might be eminent. The Chief was delighted to receive the roster and delivered it immediately to the Vice Unit. Three days later, I was advised to report to Internal Affairs as I was now under investigation for allegedly interfering with a criminal investigation. As shocked as I was, I reported to I.A. as instructed. There, I was informed that the Vice Unit had contacted my brother for additional help and discovered that I had told him not to play in the tournament.

When asked by the Internal Affairs investigator if such a conversation had transpired, my reply was something like, "Absolutely, and I would do so again. These creeps around here have the audacity to ask for my brother's help. He provides them with everything they need, and yet they expect me to feed him to the wolves by not warning him?"

I was livid. In the long run, the internal investigation cleared me of any wrong doing, stating that the police department was unreasonable in its expectation that I would not warn my brother about playing in such a tournament. The act still infuriates me some twenty years later. These administrators, who called me a friend, turned on me in an instant when they felt it was to their own political advantage to do so. Sometimes it is not the stranger about whom you must be weary, but rather that one in the organization who refers to you as a pal.

We had another manager in our organization who referred to himself as a "political rattlesnake." "Fool with me," he always said, "and you'll feel the sting of my fangs." Maybe so. But it has been my experience that a rattlesnake loose in the living room tends to put a severe damper on any discussion of animal rights. If you plan to survive organizational politics, you better be able to receive it as good as you give it, because organizational politics can sting, and sting badly, when you are on the receiving end.

Finally, some managers eventually get bitter because they think they know all the answers, yet nobody bothers to ask them any questions. Many times that's because of the reputation they have developed as being more political trouble than they are worth. People in the organization don't always take the easy way out, but neither will they automatically ignore the path of least resistance. I used to work down the hall from a peer manager who was so obnoxious, I had standing instructions with my secretary to close my door every time she heard him coming. I admit up front my impatience with his cantankerous nature, but I was generally more afraid of being seen by others in his frequent company. Managers like him have few friends in the organization. Therefore if they find someone who will tolerate them, they stick to them like a barnacle to the hull of a boat. It may be a sad commentary, but you do get politically known for the people with whom you associate.

Managers have no more chance of avoiding politics than people swimming in the ocean have of avoiding sharks. It is a reality of the job. It is still a good idea to follow the golden rule when dealing with others. But the political reality is that you shouldn't be so naïve as to expect others to follow that same rule.

★ Managing to do it right…

1. Buy into the fact that management and politics are inevitably entwined. It is virtually impossible to work as a manager and avoid jousting in the political arena.
2. Political abuse finds strength in inconsistency. Strive to be consistent in all of your management activities.

3. If you need help in making a decision, ask for it. If you've already made the decision, announce it, and stick by it. Don't play political head games with your subordinates and peers.

4. Dish out only as much political avarice as you're willing to eat yourself. Believe me, it doesn't taste like chicken.

5. Be careful with whom you associate. Your reputation is at stake.

6. Express trust in those with whom you must play political poker…but always cut the organizational cards.

CHAPTER ELEVEN

Get The Hook

"...*Regular use may provide temporary relief from pain and discomfort. However, symptoms will return, as this product cannot permanently eliminate the source of irritation.*" From the waiver on a tube of hemorrhoid medication.

Fogy (also Fogey)\'fo-ge\n 1. An old person with worn out, tired, old fashioned ideas. 2. An antiquated manager who refuses to leave.

If there is anything more pitiful than a manager who should never have been a manager, it's a management misfit who won't go away when his/her time is up. It is one of the easiest lessons that nature teaches us. Water that is continually on the move is fresh, clean, and full of life. Water that stands for extended periods is stagnant, putrid, and breeds nothing except mosquitoes. It is all too often a sad fact that the managers who contribute the least hang on the longest. It is not because they still have ideas, energy, and enthusiasm to contribute. If that were the case, this chapter would not be necessary. But some managers simply cannot let go. They need the power, the title, and the recognition so desperately that they will do anything, including suffer in silent humiliation, in an effort to hang on for as long as possible. This is not always the case. Some managers are so full of excitement that it seems they can go forever. They are smarter than the average bear and thrive on the internal struggles of the organization. They never get tired of the daily grind and are super-charged by the turmoil of the day-to-day decision-making. Managers like this are not the target of this chapter's arrow. The managers about whom I speak here are exemplified by the following story.

Buzzbert had been with his organization for years. He was a mediocre manager at best and was the butt of many a joke for the majority of his management tenure. If he excelled at anything, it was at crowing about his executive prowess and his institutional knowledge. In fact, he is the choreographer for many of the steps I spoke of in the chapter called "The Chicken Dance." Workers looked forward to his retirement and would have paid a bundle to attend his retirement party just to celebrate his passing. But, guess what? It didn't happen. He didn't leave at 25, 27, or even 30 years. He stayed and stayed and stayed—blocking the promotion of other up and comers, bottlenecking new projects, and enthusiastically contributing to the stagnation of the organization.

This is a sad state of affairs. But in some respects, the organization itself contributes to this phenomenon. Perhaps one of the most egregious violations of organizational integrity has been unintentionally committed by the creation of the "DROP Program." This is a program which allows tenured employees to continue in employment for a period of time (usually 5 years) beyond the time when they are procedurally expected to retire. The idea behind this concept was to create a way to retain for a little longer those who had worked inside the system for say 25 years, but who still had something to contribute and were not quite ready to quit the rat race and go fishing.  The essence of the idea may have been noble. And there is no doubt that it prolonged the benefit of having a few employees around who could help maintain the course and supplement organizational energy. Unfortunately, however, DROP was also very attractive to those muttonheaded managers who had nothing else to do, no where to go, and couldn't get a job waiting tables in Tijuana were they to leave. Their energy level is depleted, their only interest is in their paycheck, and their loyalty to the organization is compromised by their emphasis on self.

I attended a meeting with one of these hangers-on a few years ago. The purpose of the meeting was to determine how the State Department of Law Enforcement could be of more assistance to local law enforcement agencies. A major idea that came out of the meeting was for the State to develop a certification program for local crime scene technicians. This would train them to be better evidence collectors at crime scenes, as well as increase their credibility to testify as experts in court. The idea met with rave reviews from everyone in the meeting with one exception. Unfortunately, the exception was this well-connected law enforcement manager in the DROP program of his organization. He took the floor in vehement protest to such a certification program with the argument that if employees became more qualified, they might, in fact, deem themselves more valuable to the organization, and might dare to ask for a higher rate of pay. Further, if they didn't get a raise, they might seek to unionize, or, worse still, seek employment with a competitive agency. His entire premise was grounded in the fact that by trying to improve employee performance, we were threatening the very stability of our organizational existence. Good gosh in glory, how sick is that? God forbid we do anything to improve the performance of our employees. But that is the mentality of the "boat anchor" manager—don't move forward, don't make progress, don't do anything except circle the wagons and keep that salary flowing in.

If you are a manager who is somewhere close to this neighborhood, you should be aware of the following symptoms. Of course, you'll never read this book because you stopped thinking you needed any additional education about two decades ago. But someone will anonymously lay this on your desk, so pick it up and read it. Managers who are ready for the trash bin evidence the following:

1. **Constantly talking about the good old days**: Truth be known, the good old days are, in fact, old...and, in truth, were not as good as they are today. With few exceptions, organizations get better with age. Even the stalwarts like Ford, Westinghouse, I.B.M., and G.E. are better than they use to be. Managers with energy may briefly reflect on the past, but their emphasis is on the future. Organizations which are not moving forward are not moving at all. An effective manager does not lead by looking backwards. Strength comes from focusing forward, not by looking in the rear view mirror.

2. **Dwelling upon past achievements**: Organizational memories are short. I could talk for hours about all the things I did which, in my opinion, were important during my years as a manager. But all it would do for you as a listener is make you want to go freshen your drink. What happened in the past **is** important. It establishes a groundwork and creates a legacy which colors the organization of today. But yesterday's accomplishments do little to satisfy the appetite

of today's worker. "Those Were the Days" may have been a sweet song for Archie and Edith Bunker, but it means little right here and right now. Today's manager is only as good as what s/he is accomplishing this very minute. What happened yesterday is past, gone, kaput. If you're managing effectively, you are busy with the business of today. If you're dwelling on the past, your management rudder is stuck in the mud.

3. **Playing devil's advocate to excess:** Excuse me, but who decided that only the good ideas come from you. Just because you didn't think of it, or just because it's never been done that way before, doesn't make it a bad idea. Too many "over the hill" managers confuse years of experience with years in position. They want to question everything with which they are unfamiliar or anything which pushes the envelope of comfort. To be sure, no one should enter into anything half-cocked or unprepared. But the management ninny who sits in his/her feathered nest and shouts doubt at every new idea, has become too much at home to be useful.

4. **Inaccessibility:** The object of the game "Hide and Seek" is to find a place to hide where you cannot be found. Unfortunately, this doesn't work for managers. Management is not an absentee activity. Managers must be accessible and approachable. This is easy to talk about…it's hard to do. Very seldom will an employee approach a manager just to tell him/her how good things are and how wonderful life is. They come bearing questions, complaints,

predicaments, enigmas, and problems to be solved. Your job as a manager is to look for trouble and head right for it. Any other option is a copout, and any attitude to the contrary is the attitude of someone who should have gotten out of the business a long time ago.

5. **Failure to maintain a positive outlook**: When the going gets tough, the tough get going. Sounds good, but it is definitely not the rally cry of the tired manager. When things get hard, the tired manager generally digs a hole. Sharp managers who are still in there pitching stay sharp and focused on the organizational goals. Tired managers recite the number of months until their retirement and express little interest in the objectives or direction of the organization. I'm reminded of the couch potato who claims that, "Whenever I get the urge to exercise, I just go lay down until the urge goes away." Worn out managers started seeing the glass as half-empty a long time ago. Their engine may still hobble along, but their tank is low on gas.

6. **Failure to admit that the jig is up**: It is the key question that professional athletes continually ask. "Do I leave while I'm at the top of my game, or do I risk another season?" Good managers hear the bell when it rings. They know that they have done all they can for the organization and are willing to turn over the reigns to a younger, meaner, leaner group of heroes and heroines. Curmudgeon managers refuse to admit that it is time to get out of the way and allow the organization to march on. Instead, they hang around, making fools of themselves, and creating fodder for the water

cooler chatterboxes. They can't come to grips with their own obsolescence, and, if they do, they won't admit it. It is actually rather sad. They have outlived their usefulness and have become the organizational buffoon.

Management is hard, hard work, and eventually it takes its toll. It has been my good fortune over the years to see many managers who have done splendid management work and have led their organizations to high levels of achievement. I have also seen the opposite. Managers who have outlived their productive years do more harm than simply taking up space in the organization. They set a very poor example for subordinates, and like the wagon with no wheels, simply cause friction as they are drug along inefficiently by the rest of the organization who simply wishes they would go away.

★   **Managing to do it right...**

1. Do a periodic, honest self-evaluation of your management style to make sure you haven't lost your edge.
2. Realize that time waits for no man. Eventually, you must step aside and allow someone else to take the helm.
3. If you are telling yourself good things about your management philosophy, and your organization is saying something entirely different, maybe it's time for you to shut up and listen.

CHAPTER TWELVE

There Are Still Heroes

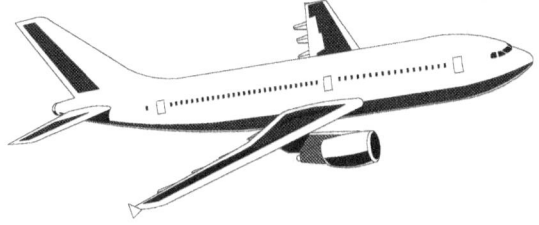

"Let's Roll" United Flight 93, September 11, 2001

Manager\'man-ij-er\n 1. One that manages.

After reading these chapters, it might be easy to conclude that everyone in management is misplaced, mistaken, and/or messed up. But that is not the case. There are still management heroes out there who come to work every day with an immeasurable amount of enthusiasm and energy, who are zeroed in on productivity, and daily exemplify the leadership skills necessary to motivate others. There is no magic to it. Good managers are not perfect. They were not born managers, nor do they possess any specific type of God-given talent which is unavailable to others. It has been my experience, however, that the managers who represent the best of the best possess certain and similar qualities which are consistent with success. I have listed them below, and believe them to be the ten commandments essential to good management.

1. **They care first and foremost about the organization.** In my book on supervision, I admonished the new supervisor to **always** make decisions based upon what is best for the organization. Nothing changes here. But, in management, the manager must sometimes make decisions which, although are organizationally best, are not even in the manager's personal best interest. It doesn't matter. The first oath of management is allegiance to the organization. If a manager places any interest above that of the company s/he serves, it is a violation of the trust which is accorded them by virtue of their position.

2. **They are people oriented**. People who don't like people simply cannot manage. By definition, managers are responsible for getting work out of others. We have a cliché in the educational arena which goes, "College work would be great if we could just get rid of the students." Maybe management would also be easier without subordinates, but such cannot be the case. Managers are not evaluated based upon what they do. They are evaluated upon what they can get others to do. Managers who do not like people are miserable. And so is everyone who works for them.

3. **They know how to listen**. I am always amazed at the number of managers who think they can learn something while their mouth is open. Good managers listen to what their employees say, listen to what they don't say, and what they would like to say, but, for some reason, can't. Call it a management sixth sense if you will, but I found very few subordinates who were unwilling to talk once given the opportunity. And I can attribute more than one management success to regularly keeping my ears open and my mouth shut.

4. **They know that they don't know it all.** "Ego" is a significant management hurdle. Regardless of what some people think, no one knows everything about everything. Everyone needs help now and then.
I am reminded of one manager with whom I worked. I am sure this guy

has poured over the Bible looking for his name because he is sure he wrote it. He obviously didn't, because he would never have written that part about, "…blessed are the meek…" Nobody likes a know-it-all, especially in management. And no manager, regardless of the level of intelligence, has all of the answers all of the time.

5. **They are willing to admit mistakes**. The only way to completely eliminate mistakes is to do nothing. Managers are humans too, and they'll make mistakes from time to time. The interesting point here is that subordinates will forgive mistakes provided the manager stands accountable and takes steps not to repeat the error. What fires up subordinates is when managers refuse to own up to errors which are directly attributed to management action. Even worse is when they attempt to lay the blame off on someone else. Good managers know they are not infallible. They try hard to do the right thing and are willing to admit it when they flub up.

6. **They make decisions**. Indecisive managers have about as much impact as a Nerf ball bouncing against a concrete wall. The manager who constantly avoids making decisions soon becomes an organizational laughing stock. The manager's job is to collect information, process that information, and then to act upon it in a timely manner. Research has proven that even wrong decisions are, many times, better than no decision. At least a wrong decision eliminates one more thing that will not work. Decisions do not always need to be made on the spur of the moment, nor do they

need to be made in a vacuum…but they must be made. Successful managers know this and act accordingly.

7. **They continue to learn**. One of the fallacies I continually see at our college is that managers rarely attend the management classes. We have plenty of up and comers who want to be managers someday. But we don't seem to attract those who have already reached the management ranks. One reason I frequently hear is that, "I don't need the training. I'm already a manager." What faulty logic. No one is dumber than the one who thinks there's nothing left to learn. Good managers don't think that way. They are always looking for some way to improve their performance. They understand that learning extends their management life and stacks the organizational chips on their side of the table.

8. **They are politically savvy**. Frankly, I do not hold the science of politics in very high esteem. However, I do think that if you run with the big dogs, a decent amount of knowledge regarding high grass is required. Successful managers know enough about the political realities of their job to survive and to flourish. They don't eat their political peas with a knife, and they carefully choose their battles. Many people categorize politics as deceit, deception, and self-interest. But the broader definition can also include advantage, control, and getting others to do what you want. The manager who can wiggle and weave his/her way through the political jungle of the organization is much more prepared to remain in the race for the long run.

9. **They understand their role.** Management is not about finally crossing the finish line. Achieving the position of manager is like commencement in college. It is a beginning. Managers who lay back and coast are as obvious as a wart on the nose. Management means work. It is a daunting, difficult, and demanding task if it is done right. Good managers know this. They not only accept the accolades, they accept the responsibility. They know their role in the organization and face it squarely and enthusiastically every day.

10. **They have talent.** I have continually said that managers are made, not born. But somewhere in their individual gene pool there must be a certain amount of talent potential. Successful managers have it, unsuccessful managers don't. Promotion to a management position is no guarantee that the person can manage. But the manager with a flair for working with others, who is willing to build upon that basic skill will eventually rise to the top, both in productivity and popularity.

★　　Managing to do it right...

1. Remember these ten commandments and constantly work to hone your skills.
2. Remember that managers are servants, not masters. Be fair, be humble, and be loyal to the organization you serve.
3. Teach your subordinates in a way that will one day make them good managers.

0-595-25603-1